JESSICA HARRIS

love done

right

REFLECTIONS

Book Formatting by Derek Murphy @Creativindie
Author photo by Vanessa Baczewski.
Cover photo by Gronde Photography.

http://www.beggarsdaughter.com

ISBN: 978-0-692-84752-7
First Edition: August 2017

10 9 8 7 6 5 4 3 2 1

...that Christ may dwell in your hearts through faith—that you, being rooted and grounded in *love*, may have strength to comprehend with all the saints what is the breadth and length and height and depth, and to know the *love of Christ* that surpasses knowledge...

Ephesians 3:17-19 (ESV)

Five Years Later

THE FIRST BOOK I EVER WROTE was not a book at all. It was 21 thoughts whipped together and published online, just in time for Valentine's Day. I was experiencing life with a joy, wonder, and profound freedom I had never known before. It felt like I had figured it out. All of it.

The years have brought wisdom and a sense of humility. There is a growing understanding that, even when I am 62, I will not know everything.

Looking back on that first little online devotional is a bit like looking at my sixth-grade yearbook photos. There I was, sporting a 1980s side-ponytail (it wasn't the 80s). I wore a white turtleneck with little black penguins all over it. If I remember correctly, I had baggy, bright, blue sweatpants on too. Thankfully, they were not pictured. It was bad.

I might have felt semi-confident at the time, though with my frizzy hair and pointy eyebrows, that is highly unlikely. Still, I am sure I thought I at least looked decent. Why else would I do that for pictures?

Two decades removed, I have to ask myself, "What was I thinking?"

It was that way with my first little e-book. For years, I never read it myself. After all, I wrote it. I already knew what it said. In fact, by the time I was done, I practically had it memorized. There was no need to read it again.

Then, one day, I sat down, read it, and thought, "Wow... if I knew then what I know now." Nothing is wrong with it (except for the occasional spelling error I can't even blame on autocorrect). There is just so much missing. That's the problem with writing about life lessons; you never stop learning them. The book you write now won't be the same as the one you would have written five years from now.

My initial thought was to pull it from the shelves and pretend it never happened. It occurred to me, though, that reflection is important. ***Imperfection*** is important.

We live in a culture of glamour and filters, retakes and Photoshop™. Our lives always seem perfect, and we can try to hide the evidence to prove otherwise. We untag, delete, use the blemish correction tool, retake, pick a different filter. Everything is perfect. There is nothing left to fix, nowhere left to change, nowhere left to grow.

⦛

We are more prone to take a selfie than we are to sit and take an honest look at ourselves.

⦛

Our worlds are so noisy and our lives so busy, we don't often take time to stop and deliberately think about anything. We fill our days with jobs, school, social media, and entertainment. We are always plugged in, stimulated, engaged.

If we think about something at all, it's usually because we are worried or obsessing about it, not because we want to learn, grow, or reflect. We are more prone to take a selfie than we are to sit and take an honest look at ourselves. Our eyes are always on what is around us.

We are little plants with shallow roots, struggling to take hold in a world that is constantly pushing us around. Deliberately hitting the "pause" button on our lives gives us a chance to grow and send our roots down deep. It also gives us a chance to see the growth so far.

Looking back can be tough, though. As we grow and heal, taking time to review the road we have traveled can sometimes be painful. There are people we have hurt along the way, people who have hurt us, lessons we have learned, and lessons we wish we would have known. Reflection is good. It encourages us to keep moving forward in pursuit of healing and it shows us the value of our redeemed pasts.

Scattered throughout this book will be pieces of the original *Love Done Right: Devos* as well as opportunities for you to document your own thoughts. When you pick it up again, you will be able to see how you have grown. Think of it like those marks on the walls at Grandma's house. Every year, you stand against the same wall of the same house, but *you've* changed, and you don't really notice until you step back and see the marks on the wall.

The woman I am now is not the same as the woman who threw together a little devotional book years ago. A journey took place in those years- a journey further into an understanding of love, with things learned not only from my own story but from the stories of women around the world.

Reflections is a sharing of that journey and an invitation for you to take your own. I'll never know it all. One of the amazing things about love is you can never know it all. It infiltrates my story, your story, and keeps calling us deeper, wider, higher, further into a love that knows no bounds, no limits, no fears.

No matter how far along you are, there will always be more to learn. There is hope, healing, and so much growth on the way.

Jessica

Broken Loves

Love anything and your heart will be wrung and possibly broken. If you want to make sure of keeping it intact you must give it to no one, not even an animal. Wrap it carefully round with hobbies and little luxuries; avoid all entanglements. Lock it up safe in the casket or coffin of your selfishness. But in that casket, safe, dark, motionless, airless, it will change. It will not be broken; it will become unbreakable, impenetrable, irredeemable. To love is to be vulnerable.

-C.S. Lewis, *The Four Loves*

*W*e all start off in this world with a blank love slate. That is not a real thing- I just made that up. Think of a newborn baby. They are wholly dependent on others for their care. They do not know what it means not to trust.

A stranger could pick up a baby and that baby will snuggle down and sleep. They smile; they attach; they connect. They do not understand people can possibly *not* love. Love and trust are natural. Distrust, fear, and hatred are learned.

A few years ago, I had the opportunity to work as a live-in nanny for my cousin. I watched her 1-year-old son and her nephew who was just four months old when I started. The littlest one, baby S, had the sweetest smile and was one of the happiest babies I had ever met.

One day, as he was still figuring out how to stand, I sat down with him on the floor. I scooped my arms underneath his and picked him up, steadying him as he plopped his little feet underneath him.

I held him, waiting until I could feel him bearing weight. Then, I let go. He would stand upright only for a split second before he started to tip over. That moment of standing always seemed to surprise him. *Wait? People do this!?*

Just as he realized he was standing, he would start to fall. I would let him go a tiny bit before I would grab him, keeping him from falling and banging his head on the floor. The belly laughs rolling from his wide, bright-eyed grin were contagious. There was a wonder, a thrill, a joy.

It became a game for him. He would start to laugh in anticipation when I stood him up. He got excited about standing up because he loved the feeling of falling (and being caught). Future adrenaline junkie in the making.

What if I had dropped him? What if I had pulled him up, let him go, and watched him fall? I doubt he would have been laughing then. What if I had let him fall and left him there crying on the floor? That would be horrible.

For some of us, that is our story with love. It was all great until something happened- someone dropped the ball, someone walked away, someone messed up. We were experiencing love as intended. Then, it broke.

Maybe your parents grew distant. Maybe they gave you up. Maybe your family is great but somebody else "dropped" you- a boyfriend, a friend. You might even feel like God dropped you. Perhaps the only person you feel ever loved you is now gone- claimed by some tragedy, disease, or old age, and you feel left behind and alone.

&

The picture we have of love suffers blow after blow. Eventually, it's a pile of shattered glass on the floor.

&

Love goes from being safe and beautiful to broken and dangerous. We are hurt. We are wounded. We are scared. We stop trusting and start suspecting. The picture we have of love suffers blow after blow. Eventually, it's a pile of shattered glass on the floor. We push back, isolate ourselves, and wait for the hammer to drop again.

When love gets broken, we get hurt. We hate talking about it because no one likes feeling like damaged goods. However, if we do not take the time to clean up that broken glass, we spend our lives suffering scrapes, cuts, and wounds.

We never look at love the same again. It becomes suspect. We become defensive or desperate, shallow or suspicious. We may even try to convince ourselves love does not exist. After all, we thought we had it once, and now it is gone.

Maybe love is not broken for you. Perhaps it is cracked a little, or foggy. You do not have to have a trauma to struggle with seeing love clearly.

In their book, *The Sacred Romance*, authors John Eldridge and Brent Curtis talk about the message of the arrows. The arrows are things contrary to love, things that would seek to hurt us.

When it comes to those arrows, our lives might seem like we are constantly in the climax of an adventure movie. We live non-stop in the fight scene, fending off one bad guy after another with our slow motion martial arts, cat-like reflexes, and gold medal swordsmanship.

Every day, every relationship, we are dodging arrows fired from a thousand skilled marksmen. We are immersed in a new drama, wondering when it is all going to end and we can live a "normal" life. Maybe marriage, or maybe good friends, maybe moving out of home, maybe more money... *something must fix this!*

We want life to be easy like it was when we were little. We felt we could really trust and love people. We want love to be a good and safe thing. We want places where we feel secure, accepted, and whole. It is hard when the places that should be safe are not or when the places that once were safe are no longer.

That is the danger of broken loves. We all experience them one way or another. We are familiar with broken loves- love that was supposed to be there and is not, comes at a cost, or just simply stopped. We come to believe that these shabby shards are all there is, and it changes us- not for the better.

Reflections

Date: _____

What are some ways I have witnessed or encountered "broken loves?"

What are some ways my *own* love is broken? *(For instance, "I can get really mad at people I love and might say harmful things to them.")*

We live in a world filled, not just with fake loves, but with broken loves. In some sense, the broken ones are more dangerous, because they were once whole.

#LOVEDONERIGHT

Enough

Write out Romans 5:8

What stands out to you in that verse?

~

    When I was a little girl, I developed this idea love was something you had to earn. It didn't just come to you; you had to be *worthy* of it. So, I embarked on this subconscious mission to become loveable.

    When I say "loveable" I really just mean, "I did everything I could *not* to disappoint people." Love was the absence of disappointment. Love was something I deserved to lose.

    It is a message you can get from society. Love is about acceptance and approval. Love is measured by the number of likes you get on Instagram or how many followers you have on Snapchat.

Certain cultures and family backgrounds can make love feel conditional. Whether you are worthy of love can be dependent on performance. You have to get the grades. You have to win the games. You must perform!

We think that love is something we achieve. It is a goal we pursue. It is a status we earn. This leaves us in a place where we believe, in our heart of hearts, we have somehow failed at being loveable. We believe we do not deserve love and we will *never* deserve love.

We spend our lives trying to be worthy of love. It leaves us constantly seeking affirmation from people, shattered by rejection, and desperate for connection. There is no security in a love that is not sure.

Have you ever thought any of these things?

God is probably sick of me right now.

I wonder how much longer He'll put up with me.

There's no way He still loves me.

All evidence and truth to the contrary. The verse in Romans tells us He loved us even when we were yet sinners. It does not say, "Once they finally got their act together, Christ died for them."

Struggling with sin? He still loves you. He is not sitting up there keeping track of the number of times you screw up, just waiting to kick you out.

The reality of love is that it loves us in spite of ourselves. The love of God was such that He loved us even while we were acting against Him. Even while we were running from Him and doing everything contrary to Him, He loved us. Perfect love is given. A love that must be earned is broken.

Pause

What's one thought I can meditate on today?

Romans 5:8

I don't have to earn God's love

Or my own:

Temporary

Write out Romans 8:38

Underline the things that cannot separate us from God's love.

❧

Some of us have never known a love that never leaves. We have parents who left, husbands who left, boyfriends who dumped us, friends who deserted us. We think everyone is going to be that way. Worse, we think *God* is going to be that way.

Women and girls will write me and say, "I'm just waiting for God to walk away." We cannot believe God plans on staying. Surely, there must be something we can do to tick Him off enough to make Him slam the door and never come back.

From Love Done Right: Devos

The fear of abandonment is very real. Divorce rates are rising. Infidelity is rising. We can get desperate and lie to people or disguise the truth in an effort to make sure we keep their love. Then, we are haunted by this constant paranoia of them discovering the truth. It is a very real problem.

Sometimes we are not that secure in love. We feel like there might be an invisible line that we cross, and once we cross it, love is over. We feel like we can lose love, that we can somehow fall away from it. While that may, unfortunately, be true with humans, it is not true with God.

This is why God's love is such a firm foundation for us. It is a fertile soil for us to throw down roots, take in nourishment, and grow. There is no risk of abandonment with Christ.

ى

I need to remind myself of this constantly. Being abandoned is a small part of my story, yet significant.

On a normal day, I am an extremely logical, rational, and level-headed person. Still, I get gripped with fear over random things- like when my ride is late. Even though I completely understand traffic delays and the fact some people aren't punctual, I can be overcome with fear and anxiety. I am convinced I am being deserted somewhere. It doesn't matter how much I trust the person, I believe they are done and have left me.

I have found the only thing that helps is remembering God does not leave me. People have, do, can, and will. God can, but has not, does not, and will not.

∼

Pause

Do you consider yourself loved by God? If you were honest, what is something you feel separates you from God's love?

Beautiful

Write out Psalm 139:14-15

Circle every adjective used to describe us.

When I was 17, I sent nude pictures to a stranger. To this day, it is one of the biggest regrets of my life. It was a long road that led me to that place. The moment he said, "You're beautiful," I would have done anything for him. At the time, I thought that was the price you pay for love.

So many women- young and old- get tangled up in the web of lies that says you must be sexy to be loved. That leads us on this quest to be just like the women in the movies, magazines, and even the porn films. The sexuality of women is idolized and put on display everywhere you look.

From Love Done Right: Devos

We weren't created to be sexy. We were created to be beautiful, and yes, there is a difference. We were handcrafted by God, for His purpose and His pleasure...

What if there was a billboard that said, "You don't have to be sexy to be beautiful. You don't have to be sexy to have love." What kind of hope would that billboard bring?

...

It all boils down to what message you are willing to fight for. What message does your body believe?

Do you settle for the lie that women are only good for one thing or do you choose to believe that you are worth more than a $5 tube of lipstick and a $10 mini skirt?

I once shared the story of those pictures at an event for teen girls. At the end, I encouraged them to come forward for prayer and asked if they could write what they wanted prayer for on a sticky note. One young girl came up to me with her note, sharing a story of how her boyfriend had asked for nudes. She gave them to him and then he dumped her. On the back of the note, she had written:

I FEEL SO LOST

We hear our worth and value, especially as women, depend on how sexual our bodies are. We listen to what culture tells us and feel we need to change ourselves, even sell ourselves, to find love.

Yet the message of Scripture is that our bodies, down to the most intimate details were crafted by God. Beyond that, we are told that our bodies are His temple, bought by Him (1 Corinthians 6:19-20). Your body is priceless and should never be sold for the sake of "love."

ᴂ

Pause

What is your ideal picture of beauty? Name a person if you want to be "just like them." What does that image tell you about who you are right now?

Pity

Write out 1 Corinthians 13:3

❧

Perhaps your experience with love has always been someone trying to fix you. You walk away feeling more like a project than a person, more like a puzzle in need of solving. Instead of having genuine compassion motivated by love, actions can be motivated by being uncomfortable.

Your crying makes me nervous and uncomfortable, so I am going to sit here and try to "help" but I really don't care about anything more than my own comfort and fixing this as quickly as possible. Pity can be self-serving.

I didn't understand the difference between love and pity until my second trip to Tent City, an isolated village 30 minutes outside of Manila in the Philippines. During that trip, we met a little boy with a high fever. He was inconsolable in his mother's arms, crying so hard he would stop breathing.

He was suffering from hydrocephalus (water on the brain), which made his head far too large for his body. His week-long fever was probably caused by an infection. We feared he was dying. The nearest medical care was over an hour away. While the team would typically take him to get help, we had already given the last seat away to a boy with a broken femur.

I bought a bag of ice from one of the shacks with a freezer and gave it to the young mom to press against her baby's neck. We walked away, feeling completely helpless.

The ice would have melted by the time we got back to our trucks. It gave him maybe five minutes of comfort in the sweltering tropical heat. I cried. The ice seemed so stupid. It didn't fix anything.

The week before, I had gone to a market near our team's base and bought a huge bag of vegetables to give to the village. It steamed before we got there, but still, that seemed much more significant than a melting bag of ice. At least the vegetables were nutritious. It gave them *something*. What good was a bag of water?

I wrote later that day:

> I would like to think that somehow that 10 cent bag of frozen water showed the love of Jesus. That for one moment, this mother felt some sort of hope, some sort of care, some sort of love. That she felt significant, that she

felt like she mattered, that if we could care, then God *definitely* cares.

See, that's ultimately why we're here. We are ambassadors, representing the cause of a loving God. We are His hands and feet. We are His heart to a lost and dying world. We are the cup of cold water. We are the bag of ice.

࿇

I learned that day. Love does not mean "I fix your problems" or "I fix you." Instead, love gives all, not necessarily to fix a situation, but to walk with a person through it.

࿇

Pause

Have you ever felt like a project? Can you think of a relationship or a situation that *you* would rather fix than endure?

Pride

Write out 1 Corinthians 13:4

Circle or underline all the attributes of love.

❧

Pride is a sneaky little struggle. Sometimes it is loud and obnoxious. Other times, it is subtle, quiet, and almost poisonous. Sometimes pride covers up, but so does love. Sometimes pride protects, but so does love. It is not so much the manifestation as it is the motive.

It is quite possible to exhibit all the attributes of love and be fake.

We can appear to love others but our motive could be just that- to *appear* to love others. Love isn't flashy. It doesn't go out of its way to draw attention to itself. Love doesn't blow a trumpet when it is present. Contrary to every musical, it doesn't come with a full orchestra and a dance number.

From Love Done Right: Devos

What was one of the things that real love does not have?

Pride.

We, as humans, have a natural tendency to be prideful. We boast of our accomplishments; dwell in the spotlight; soak in praise. We like us. Lust has a weird way of pumping that up while tearing us down...

Still, pride will try to protect us. We may push to excel and be noticed in other areas just so people will not wonder. We use our pride to protect the part of our life that is nothing to be proud of....

See, lust trounces through life justifying its existence and bragging of liberation, satisfaction, fun, and freedom. Love does none of that. When love walks in a room, it is a servant, not a king. It is a lamb, not a lion. In the noise of our day and all the glitz and glamour of the world, love is the soft, muted, whisper. It is a quiet constant that often goes ignored.

∾

We can grit our teeth and bear many things, especially if we think there is some praise in it for us. If

I think other people are annoying, I will ignore them in a nice way. It looks like I am being patient, but I really want them to leave me alone. Can you relate?

Maybe you know someone who only seems to love when the world is watching. Perhaps you are like that too.

That is not what the text of 1 Corinthians is saying. Love is not attributes in a checklist. It's not "if you do these things, then you are a loving person." Instead, it is, "love, by its nature, does these things." We can have all the right answers, do all the right things, and not do it out of love.

৵

Pause

List any relationships you may have or even places you serve where your motive is not love, but instead a desire to look good in front of other people.

Wrapping Up

Did you identify any other areas of "broken love" in your life (different from the ones you listed at the beginning of this section)? If so, what are they?

What are some ways you see those broken loves affecting you or ways you see your own broken love affecting others?

Of the five lead verses in this section, choose one you would like to memorize. Work on memorizing it while you do the next section.

Counterfeit Love

"We can either deaden our heart or divide our lives into two parts, where our outer story becomes the theater of the should and our inner story the theater of needs, the place where we quench the thirst of our heart with whatever water is available."

- Brent Curtis, *The Sacred Romance*

*P*erhaps you have seen this before. A friend of yours will share something on social media that has been shared a million times. It is a giveaway and it sounds too good to be true.

> *Win five free airplane tickets to Hawaii! Just like this post and comment!*

> *Take a cruise with you and a friend- we're giving 200 tickets away now!*

You can see other people are sharing, commenting, retweeting, liking, and tagging you in it, but something does not seem right.

When you look closer, you realize the page name is spelled wrong, or it has an extra punctuation mark. In other words, the page offering the giveaway is not real. It is a counterfeit. While hundreds of people are excited about their chance at a free cruise, you know not a single one of them is going to get what they are hoping for.

∞

No counterfeit barges onto the scene announcing it is not real.

∞

A counterfeit will not willingly out itself as being fake. Counterfeiters do their best to make their product look as real as they possibly can. No counterfeit barges onto the scene announcing it is not real. They will go to great lengths to recreate the real thing- copying images and old posts so it looks authentic.

When we suffer a broken love, we start to search for the real thing. Along the way, we run into so many replacements. They are all fakes-counterfeits. They feel like love or have a piece of something that looks like love, but they're still missing something. In turn, they leave *us* missing something.

The antidote for this is understanding what real love looks like. If you do not know the features and characteristics of the real thing, you have no way of knowing if something is fake.

When I first wrote *Love Done Right: Devos*, it was all about comparing lust and love. Looking back over my own journey and thinking of all the journeys shared with me, I have realized how many counterfeits are out there. It is not just porn, lust, and fantasy.

We search for love in so many places and we water it down into many different things. Love is acceptance. Love is feeling happy. Love is being noticed. Love is being liked. Love is 1,000 retweets. Love is sending him nudes so he won't leave. We look for anything and everything to help fill our hearts.

We are not lacking for suitors. Yet, we constantly walk away empty. These "loves" we chase after require so much of us- our bodies, our hearts, our time. They leave us hungrier, thirstier, and more desperate than when we first came. It's like salt water. It looks like water and if you're thirsty, it might seem like a great option. In the end, the taste is bitter, and, instead of quenching your thirst, it could kill you.

Reflections

Date: _____

How do I define "love"?

What are other words for "love"?

The name of someone who loves me:

I know they love me because:

A counterfeit love was never
real and can never do as it
promised. Like counterfeit
money, it looks right but has
no value.

#LOVEDONERIGHT

Little Lies

Write out Philippians 4:8

List two thoughts you wrestle with often.

&

Spotting a counterfeit can be tricky. This is why truth is so important. It is vital we fill our hearts and minds with an understanding of God's love. Knowing the original inside-out helps us spot the little lies in the counterfeit.

We can easily miss the subtle changes, and those make all the difference. They are so close, sometimes, it is scary. In the original *Love Done Right: Devos*, every devotional ended with a comparison statement, showing the subtle, albeit vital, differences between love and lust. I have highlighted some of them here:

Lust says: I notice you because of what you give me.

Love says: I notice you because of who you are.

Lust says: I am unstable, constantly changing. There are no promises.

Love says: I am constant, unchanging, and keep my promises.

Lust says: Sell yourself to find worth.

Love says: I value you and I give you worth.

Do you see any that stand out to you?

We allow little lies like these to sneak into our hearts. They are close enough to the truth we believe them, without questioning. Then, they inform our lives and our actions.

Often, when we think of the importance of truth, we are thinking "big" truths- like the sovereignty of God, or whether He is powerful enough to heal the sick. These are truths many of us have sang about since we were little. But the "little" truths- the ones we never sing about- matter too.

Sometimes, it's the little truths that protect us from the little lies. Little lies are dangerous. They sneak into our hearts and plant seeds of doubt. Before we know it, we are like Eve, wondering if the big truths are true after all. Then, like Eve, we linger a little too long in the lies, and, eventually, act on them.

That fruit looked good to her. It had a lot of promise. In the end, it delivered on none of the promises it made, but God delivered on every promise He made. It is important, in your search for love, to keep a weathered eye on the truth. Let the truth determine your standard for love.

∾

Pause

Think about the thoughts you wrote down. Are they lies? What are verses that can speak truth instead?.

Lust

Write out 1 John 2:16 (use the NLT, if available)

❧

From Love Done Right: Devos

In 1999, at the age of 13, I was exposed to pornography. Years before, my father left our family and my heart began a search for acceptance, fulfillment, and love. My exposure to pornography, coupled with my searching heart, created a firestorm of lust that nearly destroyed me. By the time I was 17, I was so engulfed that I seriously considered surrendering to this fire that consumed my life. I began to explore a career in the adult industry hoping it would end the struggle and forever silence my aching heart...

As time has passed, I have grown to realize my heart was twisted, seared, and broken by habits and thoughts I had developed while enslaved to lust. So twisted in fact, that I was not able to love or be loved correctly.

Lust is the ultimate viral phishing site for love. There are other counterfeits for love out there, but lust is the most powerful. Why? Because it gives you all the best benefits of love.

It gives you a sense of acceptance, hope, and belonging. It makes you feel desired. It can bring you physical and emotional pleasure, but there is a key component missing: relationship. That is the foundation for love. With lust, you get all the "feel good" without any of the substance.

Lust can alter or even destroy great relationships. It can lead us to situations we otherwise would not have placed ourselves in. It can influence our decisions and how we choose to love other people.

It manifests in many ways, from fantasizing about the boy at church and sexting your boyfriend to watching pornography or reading erotic fan fic. What can start as seemingly innocent "exploration" morphs into a determined search for satisfaction. It leaves us sexually frustrated, discontent, and "clingy." Lust seeps into our thought lives and contaminates what should be loving relationships. We fail to realize what looks like "satisfaction" is making us less satisfied, more frustrated, and despairing.

It isn't love. It's false connection. Instead of drawing us into relationships, lust views relationships as an inconvenience. We feel loved, cared for, and connected because our sexual needs or romantic needs are being "met," but in the end, it leaves us empty.

&

Pause

On a scale of 1 to 10 (with 1 being a little and 10 being a lot), how much do you feel lust influences your quest for love?

Noticed

Write out Psalm 139: 17-18

❧

Most of us would agree we want to be noticed. One of the most popular posts on my blog to date is one entitled, "What to do with Male Attention Addiction."

Male Attention Addiction is not a real medically-definable addiction. In fact, "obsession" might be a better word. The term "addiction" was used by a reader who felt she struggled with this, and it has been used by several people searching online. The point is, it describes this intense and overwhelming need to be noticed-specifically by men, but also by people in general.

There is a part of us that wants to be seen. For us, being noticed is like being cherished. It is a part of love. We want to be precious, special, and feel like we mean something to someone.

This is what can make romance so intoxicating to women. The idea of someone swooning over us, thinking about us every moment, thinking about *only* us every moment. It speaks to a very large part of our heart. It can make us go out of our way to solicit attention, and the culture around us encourages us to do this.

How many times have you posted something on social media and then sat there waiting for someone to like it, to comment, to share it? Do you get annoyed when no one does? I fall into this trap all the time.

How many times have you carefully planned an outfit, spent extra time on your hair and makeup, and waited for someone to compliment you? Isn't it deflating no one notices?

I recently got a new phone and was not able to switch over my contacts. It was depressing to go for three weeks without adding a new number because no one was texting me. (I have email and Facebook, so it is not like I was being ignored, but still).

We want to be noticed. We do not want to be a number, a nameless face. We want to be seen! When we feel unseen, we will go to great lengths to make ourselves seen.

Did you realize the God of the universe sees you? That is a big deal. The Psalmist says God's thoughts for him outnumber the sand.

More than that, His thoughts for us are precious. They are not, "Oh no. What is she doing now? How many times do I have to tell her!?" No, they are precious thoughts.

You are *cherished* by the God of the universe. Think about that.

೪

Pause

What are some things you do to get "noticed?"

How might your life change if you no longer felt you had to be noticed (think about things like clothing, social media usage, etc)?

Needed

Write out 1 Corinthians 13:5.

What is the second attribute of love listed in this verse?

❧

My second year of Bible college, I was working in a newer church, helping them with their youth group. For whatever reason, the girls from the trailer park across the street had elected me to be their small group leader.

They were tough girls- often bragging about smoking weed and stealing cars. There seemed to be a weekly fight about who was sleeping with whose boyfriend, and I never knew who the different "sides" were from week to week.

They all came from rough homes, most of them single-mother homes with moms who worked long hours just to make life work for them. I got it because it was my story- raised by a single mom who worked insane hours every week. Some days I didn't even see her. She did it because she loved me and because she cared. As a teenager, I found it easy to feel neglected, ignored, and unloved.

Perhaps that's how I ended up doing church in the trailer park. I got it. I understood the searching for love, the need to feel like my life mattered to someone. Grant you, my search motivated me to get good grades (and simultaneously get stuck in pornography). Stealing cars, doing drugs, and having babies were not options for teenage me. That's why I worked hard to hide my shock when a fourteen-year-old told me she wanted to have a baby.

"I want to have a baby because babies need you for everything. They love you."

Not every hurting woman feels becoming a mom will fix her problems, but for many of us who have experienced broken loves, we understand the desire to feel like we matter. It goes beyond just being noticed. It is being recognized for a contribution you have made. We want someone to need us.

But being needed isn't love. In fact, it's a dangerous counterfeit. An abusive boyfriend may say, "Don't leave me! I need you" and that desire to be needed makes her stay. Or, a teenage girl feels she needs a baby in order to feel loved, so she makes the choice to become a mom at 14. In 14 years, she finds herself in the same place her mom was- raising a child alone. Eventually, babies don't need you anymore. No matter what you can offer there will come a point when people won't need you anymore.

Love gives. On the other hand, need can take advantage and hurt. If you've ever been in or witnessed a codependent relationship, you have seen the damage "need" can do when it isn't love. People who love you can need you. Yes, love meets needs, and love itself is a need we all have, but love is not defined by need.

∂

Pause

Do you feel like you matter to others even when they aren't asking something of you?

Rescued

Write out Colossians 1:13-14

❧

Letter from a reader:

> Since middle school ... at night as I lay in bed trying to fall asleep, I would think of the guy I liked and play some kind of story in my head, such as me being kidnapped and the guy I liked coming to save me, or something stupid like that... I dwelled on this, and just recently I've discovered that my whole life has revolved around my desire to be loved, to be discovered as the girl of his dreams after years of not noticing me, to be sought after.

❧

It is the crux of many a fairy tale- the damsel in distress, the spinster locked away in a tower, the unwanted, unloved, overprotected, set free by a suave, handsome man (for whatever reason, commonly a prince). And all the girls in the room say, "Awww...."

There is something about not only being noticed but also being valiantly defended. It is one thing if someone sees you standing in the middle of the street. It is an entirely different thing if that person runs out into the street to push you out of the way of a speeding car. That must be love, right?

The willingness to save someone else is a component of love, but the desire to be rescued poses a problem. We can put ourselves into situations where we are constantly needing to be rescued.

Imagine you wanted to get the attention of a certain strapping young firefighter. You do the necessary "research" to figure out his shift, proceed to light your house on fire, and lock yourself in the bedroom. Sounds ridiculous, but this is what we can do *emotionally* to people.

We play the helpless damsel as a way of drawing attention and making it so people have to save us. We may lie about trouble we are not actually in. We selfishly create situations to keep the attention and focus on us.

Some girls run away from home. Others get into improper relationships. Some may self-harm or do poorly in school. From my time as a high school teacher, I saw this desire to be rescued play out in many ways.

We think it's love if someone comes and saves us, but ask yourself- if a firefighter rescues you, is it because he loves you? It's not, really. That's where the trouble is.

We set ourselves up for heartbreak when we think love is all about rescuing us. We will run away from people who truly do love us in order to find someone who will "save" us. In the process, we will find ourselves frustrated and isolated.

Is there a component of love that rescues and delivers? Yes. Is there a component of love that would jump in front of a speeding car? Yes. Should you walk in front of a speeding car to find out who loves you? No.

∾

Pause

Do you see a pattern in your own life of creating situations where you need to be rescued? Give an example.

Wrapping Up

Our world is filled with counterfeit loves, and they manifest in diverse ways. What are some ways you see counterfeit loves in your own life?

Are there relationships in your life that are built on counterfeit/false loves? What needs to happen to change that?

Perfect Love

"Love is patient and kind; love does not envy or boast; it is not arrogant or rude. It does not insist on its own way; it is not irritable or resentful; it does not rejoice at wrongdoing, but rejoices with the truth. Love bears all things, believes all things, hopes all things, endures all things."

1 Corinthians 13:4-7

If you grew up in the church, you have been singing about love since you were little. One of the first songs church kids are taught is "Yes, Jesus Loves Me." In fact, it may be the one song you know the "hand motions" for. One of the first verses you learned was probably John 3:16, "For God so loved the world..."

If we grow up with this, why is it so hard for us to understand and live in the reality of the love of God? How do little girls, belting loudly and flailing our hands, grow into cynical, sad, and frustrated women feeling scorned by the world, desperately clamoring for scraps of love and feeling unloved? More importantly, how do we find our way back?

In Luke 15 you will find the story of two sons, often known as the story of the prodigal son. A young man approaches his father and asks for an early cash out on his inheritance. His father gives him what he has requested. The son leaves home to "find himself" and wastes his inheritance on parties and a good time.

Eventually, the money runs out and his friends leave him. He ends up working on a pig farm and is so hungry he thinks of eating the husks he's feeding to the pigs. This is when he really "finds himself."

Not particularly thrilled with the idea of camping with the pigs, he decides to become a servant in his father's home. At least there, he figures he will have three square meals, a roof, and a place to sleep.

It is interesting. He doesn't think, "Wow, I remember how much Dad loved me." He isn't recalling good times or the love of his father. Perhaps he feels he has lost that love too. He decides to return, not as a son, but as a servant. The love of the father seems lost on him.

This is what happens to our view of God's love when we have broken loves and seek out counterfeits. We lose sight of the real thing. In fact, the real thing looks fake. The idea of God's love goes the way of fairy tales and the Easter Bunny. We seem to outgrow it.

It sounds great in principle, but surely it is not as good as we were taught. There has to be a catch. There has always been a catch.

≈

The idea of God's love goes the way of fairy tales and the Easter Bunny.

We seem to outgrow it.

≈

The great scandal of God's love and grace is there is no catch. The no-strings-attached love we have been chasing after has been in front of us the whole time, just waiting to change our lives. It is not found in a man, woman, or even a family, but in God- love Himself.

Some of us have found ourselves camping out with pigs or a little lost and alone. We're left wanting by all of our searching. The way we find perfect love is not by trying harder or selling ourselves, but by turning around and heading back "home." There, we come face to face with the Father's love for us.

Reflections

Date: _____

In the story of the prodigal son, we see several broken loves. Read through the whole thing (Luke 15:11-32) and you will see the prodigal son essentially uses his father and walks away from his family. But, there is another character at play- the older brother.

When the younger brother returns, the older brother gets upset with the love the father is showing for this troublesome offspring. He becomes jealous and envious and refuses to come inside, but instead, chooses to stay out in the field and pout. Which brother do you identify with, and why?

If we are not careful,
broken loves and the pursuit
of counterfeits can make
perfect love look fake.

#LOVEDONERIGHT

Broken for Love

Write out John 3:16

Write out Isaiah 53:5

At the beginning, I wrote about broken love. How loves in our lives are done wrong and shatter like glass. It could be easy, if that is your story, to feel love cannot and should not hurt us. Ever. Real love, you feel, should require nothing of us. Then, you look at the example of Jesus.

If you participate in communion or the Lord's Supper, you have probably heard time and again how Jesus, the night He was betrayed, took bread, broke it and said that it was His body, broken. Ready to have your mind blown?

Love broke love... for love.

The love of God, which is deeper, wider, and truer than any love we could ever know, resulted in the carrier of that love being broken in order to share it. It's mind-boggling, and something a lot of people have a hard time grasping when they are confronted with the love of God.

Perhaps you have never heard of God's love or had it explained to you. Even if you have, it is helpful to remember:

Not a single one of us deserves to be loved by God, we have fallen short of His glory (Romans 3:23).

Because we have fallen short of that glory, what we deserve is eternity in Hell, permanently separated from God. That is what God's holiness demands. There is a price for sin, and that price is death (Romans 6:23).

But because God loved us, He sent Jesus (John 3:16). Jesus is the One who was broken for us. He, being God, became like us, walked this earth just like we do and was tempted just like we are (Philippians 2:5-8, Hebrews 4:15). He is acquainted with our struggles, our sorrows, and our pain (Isaiah 53:3). He knows us.

When the time came, He was wrongly accused of blasphemy and crucified (John 19:17-30). He was murdered for love.

But it doesn't stop there. Three days after His death, He came back to life and now lives, interceding for us, promising us life abundant and everlasting to all who will believe on Him for the forgiveness of their sins and who will accept His love (John 3:16, Hebrews 4:14-16, 1 John 1:9).

His love was freely given to all, rescuing us from a life of bondage to sin and an eternity separated from God. It is a love we cannot earn, but we can accept (Ephesians 2:4-9).

We'll unpack that a little more in the coming lessons, but this is the perfect love. This love is the standard for us. It's the love we are searching for and the love we, ourselves, are called to.

∾

Pause

Read through the verses noted above. What part of God's love stands out to you? If you have never heard of God's love quite like this before, what is different?

For the Joy

Write out Hebrews 12:2

What motivated Christ to endure the cross?

✍

Often, we talk about love as similar to joy and happiness. If it makes us happy, we love it. If it is something we enjoy, we love it. Not only do we view love wrong, we also fail to understand what joy really is.

The way we talk, joy and love tend to refer to feelings we experience. If we are happy, that is joy, and where there is joy, there is love. Yet, when we look at the picture of ultimate love, we see a different kind of love and a different kind of joy. The Bible says the joy set before Christ caused Him to endure the cross.

From Love Done Right: Devos

He endured the cross, but it was not just death, there was shame. It was humiliation He did not deserve. Through mind-numbing pain, through the blood, through the tears, through the taunts, through the probable lapses in consciousness, He endured. There was something in His mind that kept Him from calling down all the powers of Heaven to level the entire city of Jerusalem. There was something in His heart so worth this pain that He would choose this over the pain of losing that joy.

What was that? Us.

Think about it. It was not Heaven—He already had Heaven. It was not glory—He has always had glory. It was not power, prestige, or honor. He gained nothing at Calvary. Except us. We are the only thing that Calvary could purchase and Calvary was the only way we could be purchased.

He rejoices in the fact that we are purchased. That is the joy, the final product, He was looking toward when He endured Calvary. The joy of having you was worth all of what He endured on Calvary. He died for

you. He delights in you. You are not a thorn in
His side. You are not a nuisance to Him. You are
His delight.

∾

This truth is phenomenal. Let it sink into your heart.
The joy waiting for Christ on the other side of the cross
was us! It was you. There was nothing enjoyable about
the cross itself.

He looked at you, looked at the cross, and decided
you were worth it. Beyond that, there was joy there. It
was not a begrudging, "Why do I have to save her?"
Everything He endured on the cross was motivated by
love and worth the joy of giving you freedom and a
relationship with the Creator of the Universe.

∾

Pause

Would you say your relationship with God is one
characterized by joy? Why or why not?

Forgiven

Write out Psalm 103:12

Write out Psalm 139: 8

❧

You may have never seen these two verses paired together, but bear with me while I draw a connection here.

If you have ever been on a plane, you know the sense of awe that comes over you as you ascend above the clouds. From our perspective here on earth, we are limited by horizons. If I look to the East or the West, there is a point in my vision that is the farthest point East and another that is the farthest point West.

Once you get above the clouds, up into the atmosphere, the horizons are gone. The blues in the sky blend together and it is simply endless. You can stare for miles, and there is no end to East or West.

When it comes to our sins and our shortcomings,

we can have an earthly horizon perspective. Sure, God has removed our sins as far as the East is from the West. In our minds that looks like He has taken our sins from our houses to the ocean. It's still able to be found.

Look at it from His perspective instead. The Heavenly angle knows nothing but endless ever-deepening blue. There is no farthest point East or West.

The sins that we are ashamed of, the things that make us say, "No one could love me because of this," are gone. Flung away from us into some far-off corner of the stratosphere.

But it's like one of those cheesy TV infomercials because "Wait! There's more." He doesn't just remove our sins from us, He fills all the space between here and there.

We aren't redeemed into a vacuum. He doesn't take our sins away and say, "There you go. Call me if you need me." No. The Psalmist says that if he ascends up into Heaven, God is there. If he makes his bed in the grave, God is there. Not only are our sins no longer with us, but it is as if God takes their closeness and fills it with none other than Himself.

Still, we like to carry around this old identity. We drag around our sins like they are labels we deserve to wear. We feel like we have to "pay" for them. This is the power of the Gospel and God's love in our lives- He, the only One with any right to judge us for our sins, has taken those from us and removed them.

If we let anybody down by the choices we have made, it is God. If there is anybody who would have any right to hold our shortcomings over us and rub them in our face, it would be God. But that is not what He does and it is not what love does.

Instead of shamed, we are forgiven. Not only are we forgiven, we are given new identities, far removed from the mistakes we have made. Our new identities are built on the fullness and love of God and the righteousness of Christ.

Pause

List at least one choice in your life that you feel will always "define" you.

Chosen

Write out 1 John 3:1

The love of God calls us _____.

&

Look back at the story of the prodigal son. As he contemplated going home to "his father's house," he planned on returning as a servant. He had lost his identity as child. His father was going to become his master.

But the love we see running to the son as he comes home is the love of a father, welcoming his child. It is not a businessman coming out to inspect a new hire or someone offended coming out to say "I told you so." No, it is a father, running to his son.

Even though the son thought he had lost his identity as a son, and lost the father's love, he never had.

The verse above is just one of several references to us being part of God's family- namely, His children. For those of us with dysfunctional families, there is hope and healing in this truth if we see it the right way.

We could assume that God's "family" is screwed up just like ours. Instead of finding hope and comfort, we find shame, judgment, threats. If we are honest, some of us think God's "family" *is* just like ours.

Instead of feeling like children who are lovingly adopted, we feel like we are captives. The churches and the other children of God we see around us do not help either at times. But it is important to remember, those are the broken loves. If we evaluate life through those broken loves, we're using the wrong lens. We are looking at the perfect one now, and, in perfect love, being a child must be a good thing.

Years ago, when I worked in a department store, one of my co-workers said, "You don't understand, sweetie, as a mom, you would give the beating heart from your chest for your child."

What is so uniquely powerful about God's love is it is adoptive. He does not "have" to love us. He chooses to. Beyond that, He chooses to love us not like a friend or a brother, but like a father. He doesn't simply pity us or have mercy on us, He loves us, as a Father.

Imagine you are the prodigal son. After your time with the pigs, you decide to run to the home of this man who you know is a good man. You will work for him and know he will keep you safe. That's all you're really expecting of him. You got yourself into this mess; you don't expect him to care about you.

However, instead of hiring you, he signs you into his will and welcomes you into his home. You did nothing to deserve it. In fact, you've probably done many things that would say you do not deserve it. Still, he welcomes you, loves you, and cares for you as one of his own.

This is the case with God's love. You don't deserve it at all. Yet, He loves you as a child.

∾

Pause

Take a look at Romans 8:16-17. Who is confirming with us that we are God's children? Why is this such a powerful truth?

Surpassing

Write out Ephesians 3:19

In 1923, Frederick Martin Lehman penned the words to a classic hymn, "The Love of God is Greater Far." The third stanza of the song was adapted from an old poem, "Hadamut", written in Germany in the 11th century. The hymn sings:

> Could we with ink the ocean fill, and were the skies of parchment made,
>
> Were every stalk on earth a quill, and every man a scribe by trade,
>
> To write the love of God above would drain the ocean dry.
>
> Nor could the scroll contain the whole, Though stretched from sky to sky.

If you think you have your mind wrapped around God's love, you need to think again. His love is unfathomable. I could write this book, you could write a book, everybody could write a book, and we still could not expose the depth and height of the love of God.

It's like the night sky. I grew up in the country, where there was very little "light pollution" at night. As the sky grew dark, millions of stars would seemingly pop up out of nowhere. The harder I looked, the more I saw. Pretty soon, the expanse of it was too much to comprehend. Did you know our galaxy has 100 billion stars?!

There is no way I could ever see every star and know every star by name (oh, but God does!- see Psalm 147:4). Still, a wonder drew me in. I would never be able to know it all, but I knew I wanted to know it more.

The love of God is endless, immeasurable. If anything should blow our minds it is the love of God. Yet, too often, we let culture, life, (or even books!) shove God's love into a box. Since we cannot understand it, we get frustrated and walk away. Because it does not fit in our box, we throw it out. We grow impatient, not wanting to explore its depths. *What is the point,* we think, *I will never know it all.*

Just because you can never understand it all does not mean you should never know it at all. Just because it is too big, too high, too deep, too wide, does not mean it is unapproachable. On the contrary, the unknowable love of God beckons us in not simply to know it but to experience it. It is like no other love we have experienced before and we could spend a lifetime trying to know its depths.

≈

Pause

Look at Ephesians 3:19 again. What happens to us as we experience the immeasurable love of God?

Wrapping Up

The love of God can never be fully understood no matter how many books you read or songs you sing, but what are you doing to continue to learn about that love?

List five ways you have witnessed God's love in your own life this week.

Love Done Right

"In this the love of God was made manifest among us, that God sent his only Son into the world, so that we might live through him. In this is love, not that we have loved God but that he loved us and sent his Son to be the propitiation for our sins. Beloved, if God so loved us, we also ought to love one another. No one has ever seen God; if we love one another, God abides in us and his love is perfected in us."

-1 John 4: 9-12

It could be tempting to stop right here. It feels good, right? You understand there are broken loves and the counterfeit loves are nothing compared to the real love God has for you. From the time we were little, we have stopped there:

> Yes, Jesus loves me. Yes, Jesus loves me. Yes, Jesus loves me! The Bible tells me so.

> I am so glad that Jesus loves me, Jesus loves me, Jesus loves me. I am so glad that Jesus loves me. Jesus loves even me.

While these children's songs are true, they fall short of real, transformative truth. Yes, Jesus loves you.

He loves you with a deep, unfathomable love that passes all understanding. The next question you need to ask is "so what?"

Love calls us to action. It is not a feeling. It is something you do. Doing love right goes beyond simply understanding you are loved. That is only half of it. The other half is what that love does to you. It doesn't leave you where you are. It changes you and calls you to love.

As I was recovering from pornography, grasping God's love for me was a huge part of my healing. Over time, I found freedom and healing are different. Freedom came when I stopped doing a behavior or holding on to a grudge. But healing came when I began purposefully living love out.

Make no mistake, it is not easy. Nor is it always romantic.

There is nothing romantic about confessing your sins, faults, and struggles. It does not "feel like love" when you open yourself up to be vulnerable and pour yourself into people who could just walk away. It is scary to fully invest yourself in a relationship knowing the other person, regardless of who they are, doesn't have to stay.

We are in good company with Jesus. The love that led Him to Calvary wasn't filled with warm fuzzies either. His love led Him to be shamed, humiliated, misunderstood, mistreated, forsaken, abandoned, and, eventually, killed.

The life of love we are called to is a life of agape love. It is a life of sacrifice and surrender. A life where you pick up the cross and follow Love- identifying with shame, the struggle, the betrayal, the loss, and the brokenness of Calvary.

≈

The life of love we are called to is a life of agape. It is a life of sacrifice and surrender.

≈

Part of our struggle is when we grasp God's love, we only have a hold of it with one hand. We still are not sure if it is a love worth living for.

Maybe there is another love that is not as uncomfortable and messy. Maybe there is something we can mix in and just half-and-half it with God's love. We want all the benefits but not necessarily all the perceived risk.

Reflections

Date: _____

When you think about loving someone else, what aspect of that do you struggle with the most?

Fill this in:

I feel that if I love God, then He will _____

_____

_____

_____

I have a hard time loving others when they _____

_____

_____

The love of God does not
end at "Yes, Jesus Loves Me."
It is meant to infiltrate and
motivate our lives.

Changed

Read Philippians 1:9-11. Write out verse 10. This is the "end goal."

⁊

In 2008, I accepted a position as a high school teacher, teaching math at a small Christian school. In 2008, I was also a hot-headed control freak trying to teach a roomful of teenagers. I'll leave it up to your imagination how that went down.

It wasn't long before I heard rumors about a petition going around to get me fired. One of my students informed me of it in a rather heated exchange. "Oh yeah, Miss Jessica! Well, a bunch of the kids and our parents want you fired. It's true. There's a petition."

I went to my boss, humiliated, afraid, and honestly, confused. I only wanted what was best for my students. I wanted them to succeed, to try their hardest, and do their best. She looked at me and said, "Don't worry about it. This school isn't a democracy."

That day, there was a realization in my mind. There must have been a disconnect between the love and concern I had for my students and my ability to show it. It was clear they weren't getting the message, and I had a choice.

I could continue to act the way I had been acting, justifying myself by saying it's just my personality, I'm the teacher, and they need to get over it. Or, I could change. Love changes people- both the lover and the loved.

Because my boss cared about me, because she loved me, and because she loved the kids, she began to point out areas in my life that weren't quite right. Because I loved the kids and wanted them to understand I loved them, I changed.

That makes it sound like a simple process, but it was far from it. Many nights, I cried myself to sleep because I was so frustrated with my apparent inability to communicate care clearly.

The hard work, the refining, the iron sharpening iron brought change. The last year of teaching students who had once petitioned to have me fired would willingly come up to my desk to get study help. Study help always turned into helping them with life- with boyfriends, with family drama, with future plans.

Sometimes we think that love leaves us alone. *If you really love me, let me have what I want. If you really love me, you would accept me as I am. You would leave me alone.* Sometimes, love is demonstrated by *not* giving us what we want.

The love of God calls us to change. It loves us all the way through- from the before to the after. Like a parent wouldn't leave their child playing in a busy street, the love of God cannot leave us broken. It calls us to growth, healing, and change. That can be hard, and it may not feel like love, but it is.

ლ

Pause

What is one area where you have seen growth in your life because of God's love?

Heart

Write out 1 John 4:10-11.

How does this verse explain love?

&

Have you noticed how we fling around the word "love?" You love your friend's hair. You love that music. You love pizza. We all love chocolate.

Now, we "heart" everything. It used to be that you just "liked" things, but now you "heart" it. It's like we got tired of hearing ourselves saying we loved everything. We heart puppies. We heart our friends. We heart Jesus.

I had a professor in Bible college who would get after my classmates and me all the time for saying we loved chicken patty day. Seriously though, chicken patty day was the best day. We all looked forward to it for reasons I don't quite remember.

This is the reality of college- sitting through your last morning class, trying to pay attention to the professor when you know it's chicken patty day.

"You cannot love chicken patties," he would say, his white mustache twitching under his nose. "You cannot have covenant loyalty with chicken patties."

As much as we wanted to roll our eyes and say, "You know what we mean," in a sense, he was right. When we toss around the word "love" it loses a bit of its meaning.

It's hard to feel special when your friends love you *and* shopping. It's hard for a woman to feel loved if her husband loves her and the nachos she made for the game. We use "love" as a synonym for "enjoy." The problem with enjoyment is it changes.

I may enjoy shopping when I'm shopping for new clothes but I may not enjoy shopping if I'm shopping for Christmas presents. If I say I love shopping and then turn around and say I love you, it leaves you wondering if my love for you also "depends."

The love God has for us is drastically different. He doesn't "heart" us. He died for us. His heart *stopped* for us. No warm fuzzies. There was nothing enjoyable about that process, and yet, we recognize it as love.

So, love, then, goes deeper than just enjoying or liking something. The love God demonstrated for us was a sacrificial and covenant love that not only loved us first but also loved us to death.

If that is love, then odds are, none of us truly *love* shopping or chocolate ice cream. Who would die for chocolate ice cream?

In fact, many of us probably don't love people like that either. If that is love, and if that is the same love we are called to show to others, you, like I, probably have a long way to grow.

ॐ

Pause

How would you describe your love for others? Does it depend on what they can give you? Does it change based on how they make you feel? Is it conditional?

Casting Out Fear

Write out 1 John 4:18

What cannot coexist with love, and why?

❧

Did you know even when you do love right it can still hurt? We are broken people trying to love other broken people, and, along the way, someone is going to mess this up. To be truthful, that can be terrifying.

"What if I invest all this time into this relationship and he leaves?!" "What if I tell her everything and she goes and tells someone else!?" "What if I am honest and they want nothing to do with me anymore!?" "I am so tired of being hurt."

The path to our love can start looking a bit like the airport security checkpoint. Please remove your shoes, jackets, belts, scarves, and sweaters. Empty your pockets, remove your laptop, place it in a separate bin. Then stand in this little machine with your arms in the air. If it doesn't like you, we'll have to pat you down.

We can get like that with people. Out of fear, we push back, defend, and make life miserable for them to make them prove they are safe to love. That isn't love talking at all. That is fear.

Love is not reserved for a handful of special people in my life who pass a rigorous screening process. Intimacy on the other hand, which is where I let people into my life, is a little different.

Love is supposed to be a defining characteristic of my life and how I interact with others. That means I might get hurt... a lot. It isn't the most comforting thing to realize!

I often suspect part of the reason I am still single is because I was so afraid of being hurt. It took a while to realize love means pain. There is going to be loss, disappointment, and grief.

Whether we live a long life and say goodbye at the end, or whether the ones we love walk away, there is pain. Love hurts, not in an abusive way, but in a sense that love opens you up to feel the pain of loss and rejection. Faced with the choice, we ask ourselves if it's worth it. *Is it really worth it to love this person if some day they might be gone? Is it really worth it to let them love me?*

This is the ease and lure of things like pornography, lust, and fantasy. It's a way for us to experience emotional and physical pleasure absent of the pain and risk that comes with relationships- even friendships. I get it. It is far easier for me to imagine a life with a great guy than it is to risk hoping for one.

Fear, then, is somewhat the opposite of love. Love says, "I would die for you no matter what, even if you don't deserve it," while fear says, "I'll be in relationship with you as long as you don't ask me to die for you." It can be present in our families, our friendships, romantic relationships and even our relationships with God. One of the attributes of perfect love is that it is unafraid.

Pause

Think of one relationship in your life where fear is present. What could you do today to cast out that fear?

Letting Go

Write out 1 Peter 4:8.

↜

One of the attributes of love, and we see this clearly in Christ's love for us, is the decision to forgive. This is perhaps the hardest aspect of love for me to express. Many of you might be able to identify with that. When we are hurt by broken loves, it is easy for us to hold onto that pain.

Love heals. It doesn't necessarily erase. Love cannot change facts that have happened to you. Love cannot change the fact your parents are divorced or that you were raped. It cannot change the fact you may have made wrong choices. Love does, however, enable us to let go.

A friend of mine works with child sexual abuse victims and, one night, he and I were discussing the trauma of the stories he has heard. He said, "It makes me not trust anyone. I see a dad with his daughter and I wonder. There are these scabs, these wounds, and I'll never be able to live without them."

We talked about the difference between scabs and scars. Yes, the stories we hear change us. The things that happen to us change us. They impact our lives, but they don't have to keep hurting. Scabs can heal. They may leave behind scars and we're never going to be exactly who we were before, but can be healed.

This verse touches on a beautiful aspect of grace. If I love someone, it gives me the ability to extend them grace. If I love someone else the way God has loved me, I have no choice but to extend them grace.

One of the most healing experiences of my life was the opportunity I had to tell my father I forgave him. After decades of silence, he e-mailed me one day. I was 21 and had been praying for years for the opportunity to tell him I forgave him. I didn't want him back. I didn't want a relationship with him. Those years and that relationship, I knew, were lost. Still, I prayed for the opportunity to show Him grace.

After I got his e-mail, I told him he was forgiven. That forgiveness rippled through my life into so many other relationships. If I forgave him, then I had a harder time holding his failures against someone else. I started to heal, and, because I had forgiven him, I found myself more willing to trust and love others.

If you've ever caught yourself in a situation where you want to cry out, "I knew it, you are just like the others," it's possibly because you haven't let go of a broken love. They may not be sorry, and they may never know the pain they have caused you. They may never ask for forgiveness, but you can still forgive and find healing.

༚

Pause

Is there a broken love from your life that you just can't stop thinking about? List out ways that may be impacting your current relationships.

While we're here, I want to encourage you to remember: going through this study isn't meant to be a substitute for solid counseling. If you have endured a trauma that has left you shattered and broken, there is no shame in seeking help. Take your list above with you to your first meeting.

Fighting Back

Write out Lamentations 3:22-23. (Hint: Lamentations is in the Old Testament)

❧

Maybe it is just me, but there are days when I read a verse, take John 3:16 for instance, and it reveals some great truth about God's love and my heart's response is, 'No thank you, God, I don't feel like being loved today."

God is so constant, and I am over here constantly changing what I want. There are days when I feel I can't make up my mind. I want to be loved, but I don't want to be hurt, so there's a push and pull that happens.

For many of us, we see God's love (and even the love of others) as too good to be true. We approach the promises of God like a letter saying we have won the lottery when we haven't even played.

Sure, it sounds great, but what is the catch? Is it real? Is there a camera somewhere that will make me into a huge spectacle when I react?

When I do that, I am essentially stopping right where I am on my journey of freedom, plopping down and saying, "No thank you, I'm free enough. I'll just stay right here." I am realizing just how toxic that attitude is.

Is it enough to just be done with fake loves? Am I content just to not be addicted to lust anymore or do I want the abundant life promised to me by Christ?

That is the life He came to give but it does not come without its share of adjustments (at least not in my experience). I know I would be much better for the journey if I would take Him at His word, trust Him, and let Him do what He is doing. It is easier to cry out in pain and run.

We do the same with people! Accountability partners who get too close can quickly find themselves on the chopping block. In some ways, we would rather be alone and miserable than known and loved.

Personally, there are times when if I even *feel* a relationship is threatened, I will cut it off to protect myself. It's the old "you can't fire me, I quit" approach.

The moment a relationship or a road looks like it's going to get hard, I want to quit.

Instead of bondage to lust, we will find ourselves in bondage to fear if we do not keep our freedom in perspective. The good news is, God's love and Christ's perseverance go hand-in-hand. We know that He is going to stick with us as we grow and heal. He desires our healing.

Do not bite the hand that loves you or fight the grace that frees you. Do not question the steadfastness of God and the patience of His love. Let it accomplish what it intends to in your life. Allow yourself to know His love.

Pause

Write out Philippians 1:6

What can we be confident in?

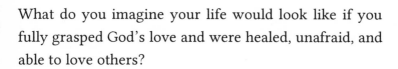

What do you imagine your life would look like if you fully grasped God's love and were healed, unafraid, and able to love others?

How is that life different from the one you have now?

List five things you can do to begin to grow in God's love.

Love is a verb

Most of this book has addressed love as a noun- an idea, a concept, a motivation. It is an experience, something we encounter, an emotion. But love, is also a verb. It is action. It is not only something done to you, it is also something you are called to do.

In 2004, a year after I graduated high school, I was at a friend's graduation party when the phone rang. When the call was over, my friend's mom announced that one of my elementary school friends had been killed in an auto accident.

I write about Darci's death often, because it is a pivotal moment in my life. The fact that it *is* pivotal explains *why* it is pivotal, if that makes any sense.

Darci actively loved people. It wasn't a "sure I'll tolerate you if you come over" kind of love, but a "let me figure out how to make sure you know how important you are to me" love. Darci was like that with everyone.

I had spent my whole life up to that point trying to make people happy. I was willing to settle for people being impressed, honestly. Love was unthinkable and I did not feel I had the capacity to love people. I felt like a fake, and fraud, and firmly believed in my heart that God could not love me. I was convinced I was unlovable and, therefore, incapable of loving others.

As I sat in Darci's memorial service, the pastor said something that struck me, changed my life and stayed with me throughout the years. He said some people spend their lives trying to impress people and it's nearly impossible to get someone to show up to their funerals. Yet, he continued, Darci spent her life loving people and the walls could not contain the lives she had touched.

Darci was only 22 when she died, but her life had impacted hundreds of people. It wasn't because she had good grades or a beautiful voice. She changed people's lives because she loved them. She made a difference in the world by making a difference in individual lives.

I prayed one simple prayer that day: "Make me like Darci." I recognized what changes people, and makes the largest impact is not your grades, your body, or how long you go to college. It's how you love.

When your last day comes, and it could be when you're 22, or 30, or 60, or 120, you might leave behind accomplishments, statistics, degrees, books, scientific discoveries, world records, whatever your dreams were.

Your eulogy might sing your praises as you climbed mountain after mountain in search of worth and something that matters. The only legacy that doesn't gather dust, rot, and fade away is a legacy shaped by love of God and love of others. These are our two greatest commandments.

We are love ambassadors to a broken world filled with broken loves and desperate for a love done right. They will never find it and never see it if we are not showing it to them.

When we know we are loved, we live like we are loved. That means we love others, not out of force but because love, by its nature, is shared. Withholding love is the exact opposite of love. Withholding love is precisely how love gets broken in the first place.

It is a circuit- as God loves you, you love others and encourage others to love God. Love must be shared. Paul talks about this when he says the love of God compels him.

Your journey does not end here- it starts here. It may take time. It may be painful. It hurts when you dress wounds. There is a lot we all have left to learn. Loving others will challenge you, and change you in ways you could have never imagined. When you have not seen real love in action, it can be hard to know what real love in action looks like, but the best teacher is Love itself.

God's love is, above all else, a call to action. It is a call to do something. Being loved makes you love.

We are here to show a world love done right.

Acknowledgments

The original *Love Done Right: Devos* was dedicated to a couple in my life who was foundational in my healing and understanding of love, Steve and Sandy. You opened your home and your hearts to a defensive, angry soul. You loved like Jesus, and I am forever changed.

The growth between now and then, I think is in part to the people God has brought into my life. People I am blessed to love and be loved by:

My small group... you are some of my dearest friends, roller coaster buddies, and supporters, even bringing me food during writing seasons (Loriel!). You keep me grounded. It's a privilege to love and take on life with you.

Every woman who, over the past eight years, has sat across from me with tear-filled eyes, sharing your story... thank you. It is an honor to be part of your stories. You are so brave.

Anne... an answer to prayer in just the perfect season. Thank you for keeping me on track. Let's go dance in the rain!

Abby, Mary, and Bambee... cheerleaders and fellow dreamers who believe in dreams bigger than I would ever dare dream. Your prayers keep the fire going.

Hannah... one of God's greatest gifts and a living testimony of hospitality. Thanks for the sushi and red bean ice cream!

My fellow ladies in the fight... this isn't a "porn" book per se, but we know that is only part of this battle. It is a joy to fight beside you for our sisters in chains.

Most of all, I must acknowledge my Lord and Savior, Jesus Christ. Without You, there is no way we could ever hope to get this right. Thank You for loving us, walking this road with us, saving us from ourselves, and for continuing to call us to a deeper understanding and a purer love. Thank You for being Love.

About the Author

JESSICA HARRIS is a self-published author, blogger, and international speaker. In 2009, she launched beggarsdaughter.com where she addresses issues of sexual addiction, lust, and singleness among women in the church. Noted as a leading voice in women's sexual struggles, specifically with pornography, lust, and abstinence, it is her heart's desire to see women of all ages find safe places in their local church where they can struggle, find freedom, heal, grow and live lives of abundant love and grace.

In 2016, she released her memoir, _Beggar's Daughter_. It is a candid account of her story of porn addiction and subsequent freedom. She now travels around the world, sharing her story, training leaders in how to help women who struggle and encouraging young people to live lives of sexual integrity in a tech-savvy and pornified world.

When she's not writing, or thinking about writing, or speaking about what she is writing, she enjoys making pretty food and being outdoors. She currently lives just north of Washington DC in Maryland with her five birds and a formidable loose-leaf tea collection. You can follow her on Facebook, Twitter, and Instagram.

For more information, visit her website:

beggarsdaughter.com

BEGGAR'S
DAUGHTER

Jessica Harris

CPSIA information can be obtained
at www.ICGtesting.com
Printed in the USA
BVHW070536010219
539209BV00002B/295/P

9 780692 847527